NICKELBACK
SHEET MUSIC ANTHOLOGY

Alfred Music Publishing Co., Inc.
16320 Roscoe Blvd., Suite 100
P.O. Box 10003
Van Nuys, CA 91410-0003
alfred.com

ISBN-10: 0-7390-6181-X
ISBN-13: 978-0-7390-6181-7

WWW.NICKELBACK.COM
WWW.ROADRUNNERRECORDS.COM

Cover Photo: © 2008 ROADRUNNER RECORDS
Album Art: *Silver Side Up* © 2001 The All Blacks B.V. • *The Long Road* © 2002 The All Blacks B.V.
All the Right Reasons © 2005 The All Blacks B.V. • *Dark Horse* © 2008 The All Blacks B.V., © Corbis Corporation.

CONTENTS

FAR AWAY

Gtr. in Drop D, down 1/2 step:
⑥ = D♭ ③ = G♭
⑤ = A♭ ② = B♭
④ = D♭ ① = E♭

Lyrics by CHAD KROEGER
Music by NICKELBACK

Moderately slow ♩ = 84

Guitar → Cmaj7 Gsus Am7 F⁶/₉

Piano → Bmaj7 F♯sus G♯m7 E⁶/₉

Verse:

Cmaj7 Gsus Am7 F⁶/₉

Bmaj7 F♯sus G♯m7 E⁶/₉

1. This time,___ this place,___ mis-used,___ mis-takes.
2. On my knees,___ I'll ask___ last chance_ for one last dance._

Cmaj7 Gsus Am7 F⁶/₉

Bmaj7 F♯sus G♯m7 E⁶/₉

___ Too_ long,___ too late._____ Who was I___ to make_ you_ wait.
___ 'Cause with_ you_ I'd with-stand___ all of hell___ to hold_ your_hand.

Keep breath - ing.___

Hold on to me___ and nev - er let me go.___

Keep breath - ing.___

Hold on to me___ and nev - er let me go.___

FEELIN' WAY TOO DAMN GOOD

Gtrs. in Drop D tuning:
⑥ = D ③ = G
⑤ = A ② = B
④ = D ① = E

Lyrics by CHAD KROEGER
Music by NICKELBACK

missed you so much_ that I begged_ you to fly___ and see____ me._
for - ty-eight hours_ I don't think_ that we left my ho - tel____ room._
3. *See additional lyrics*

You
Should

must - 've broke down_ 'cause you fi - nal-ly said_ that you would.____
show you the sights_ 'cause I'm sure_ that I said_ that I would.____

But
We

Feelin' Way Too Damn Good - 6 - 1
33229

14

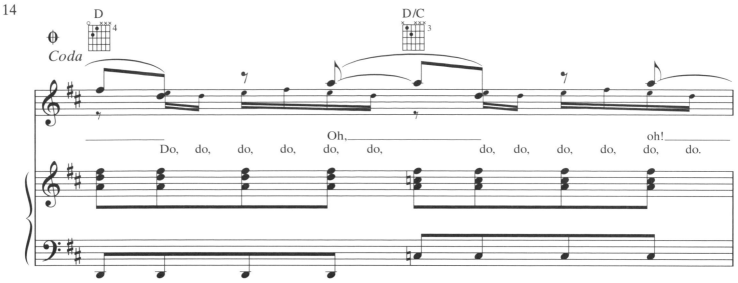

Oh, _____ oh! _____
Do, do, do, do, do, do, do, do, do, do, do, do.

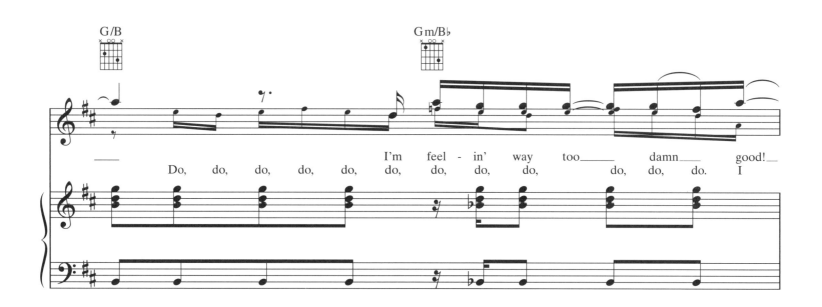

_____ I'm feel - in' way too_____ damn_____ good!
Do, do, do, do, do, do, do, do, do, do, do, do. I

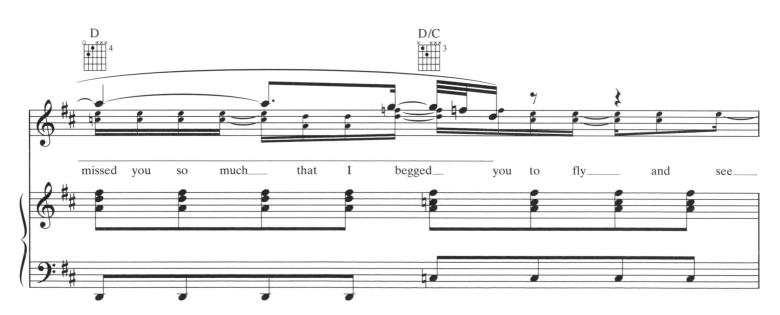

missed you so much_____ that I begged_____ you to fly_____ and see_____

Verse 3:
Sometimes I think best if left in the memory.
It's better kept inside than left for good.
Looking back each time they tried to tell me.
Well, something's gotta go wrong,
'Cause I'm feelin' way too damn good.
(To Chorus:)

FIGURED YOU OUT

Gtr. in "Drop D" tuned down 1 whole step:
⑥ = C   ③ = F
⑤ = G   ② = A
④ = C   ① = D

Lyrics by CHAD KROEGER
Music by NICKELBACK

Moderately ♩ = 96

just to fig-ure you__ out.__ Now__ I did, you won-der why.

1.

2.3.

N.C.

2. I like the freck-les on__ your chest__ Why not__ be-fore? You did-n't try.

To Coda ⊕

Gone__ for good and this is it.

Interlude:

3. I like your pants_ a-round_ your feet_

HOW YOU REMIND ME

Drop D tuning: ⑥ = D

Lyrics by CHAD KROEGER
Music by NICKELBACK

Moderately slow ♩ = 86

Verse:

1. Nev-er made it as a wise man, I could-n't cut it as a poor man steal-in'.
2. *See additional lyrics*

Tired of liv-in' like a blind man, I'm sick of sight with-out a sense of feel-ing.

Omit 2nd time

And this is how___ you re-mind___ me. This is how___ you re-mind___

How You Remind Me - 5 - 1
33229

Chorus:

It's not like you to say sor-ry. I was wait-ing on a dif-f'rent sto-ry. This time I'm mis-tak-en for hand-ing you a heart worth break-ing. And I've been wrong, I've been down, been to the bot-tom of ev-'ry bot-tle.

Verse 2:
It's not like you didn't know that.
I said I love you and swear I still do.
And it must have been so bad.
'Cause livin' with me must have damn near killed you.
This is how you remind me of what I really am.
This is how you remind me of what I really am.
(To Chorus:)

GOTTA BE SOMEBODY

Lyrics by CHAD KROEGER
Music by NICKELBACK

Moderately ♩ = 120

Ah,_____ ah ah ah ah ah ah,_____ ah ah ah

ah ah ah,_____ ah ah ah ah ah ah ah ah ah.

Verses 1 & 2:

1. This_____ time, I won-der what it feels_____ like_____

Gotta Be Somebody - 8 - 1
33229

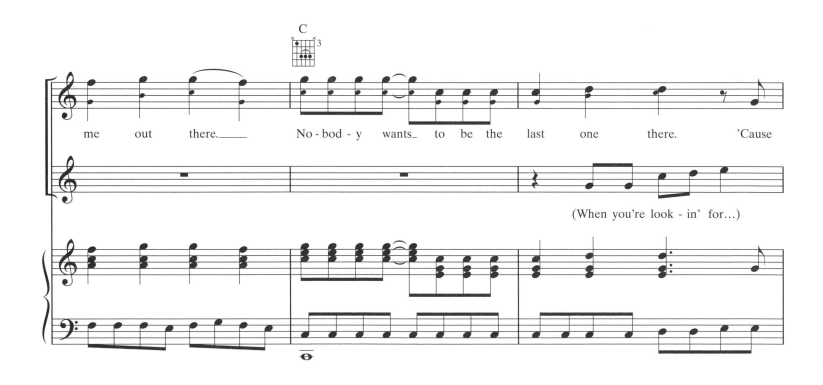

I'D COME FOR YOU

Words and Music by
CHAD KROEGER and MUTT LANGE

Moderately slow ♩ = 76

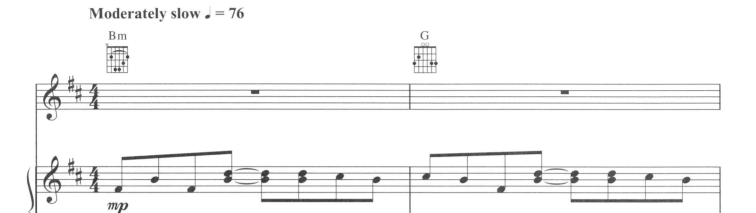

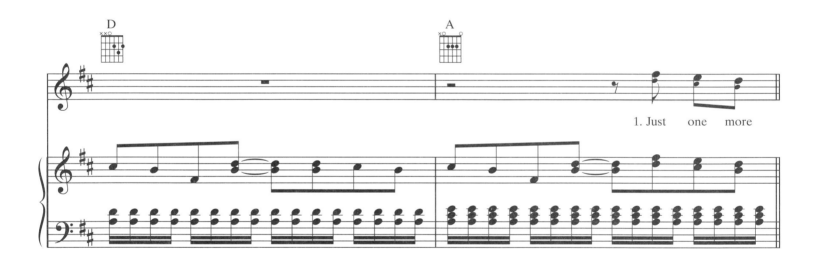

1. Just one more

Verse :

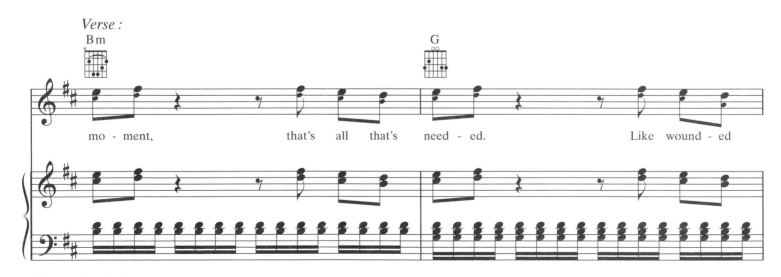

mo - ment, that's all that's need - ed. Like wound - ed

I'd Come for You - 7 - 1
33229

Chorus:

IF EVERYONE CARED

Lyrics by CHAD KROEGER
Music by NICKELBACK

Gtr. in Drop D tuning:
⑥ = D   ③ = G
⑤ = A   ② = B
④ = D   ① = E

Verses 1 & 2:

we watch the sky,___ con-fus-ing stars___ for sat-el-lites.___ I nev-er dreamed_
(2.) the fire - flies,___ our on-ly light___ in par-a-dise.___ We'll show the world_

that you'd be mine,___ but here we are,___ we're here to-night.⎫ Sing-ing,
that they were wrong,___ and teach them all___ to sing a-long.⎭

If Everyone Cared - 5 - 1
33229

NEVER GONNA BE ALONE

Moderately slow ♩ = 69

Verse:

Words and Music by
CHAD KROEGER and MUTT LANGE

Chorus:

PHOTOGRAPH

Lyrics by CHAD KROEGER
Music by NICKELBACK

Gtr. tuned down 1/2 step:
⑥ = E♭   ③ = G♭
⑤ = A♭   ② = B♭
④ = D♭   ① = E♭

Moderately slow ♩ = 76

Verse:

1. Look at this pho-to-graph,___ ev-'ry time I do, it makes me laugh.___

How did our eyes get___ so red?___ And what the hell is on Jo-ey's head?___

___ And this is where I___ grew up,___ I think the pres-ent own-er fixed it up.___
2. Re-mem-ber the old___ ar-cade?___ Blew ev-'ry dol-lar that we ev-er made.___

ROCKSTAR

Moderately slow ♩ = 76   *Verse 1:*

Lyrics by CHAD KROEGER
Music by NICKELBACK

1. I'm through with stand-ing in line___ to clubs I'll nev-er get in, it's like the bot-tom of the ninth and I'm nev-er gon-na win. This life has-n't turned out quite_ the way I want it to be.___ _ (Tell me what you want.) I want a brand-new house on an ep-i-sode of Cribs, and a bath-room I___ can play base-ball_ in.___ And a king-size tub big e-nough for ten_ plus me.

Verse 3:
I wanna be great like Elvis, without the tassels,
Hire eight bodyguards who love to beat up assholes.
Sign a couple autographs so I can eat my meals for free. *(I'll have the quesadilla, ha, ha.)*
I'm gonna dress my ass with the latest fashion,
Get a front-door key to the Playboy mansion.
Gonna date a centerfold that loves to blow my money for me. *(So how ya gonna do it?)*
I'm gonna trade this life for fortune and fame,
I'd even cut my hair and change my name.
(To Chorus:)

SAVIN' ME

Lyrics by CHAD KROEGER
Music by NICKELBACK

SHOULD'VE LISTENED

Gtr. in "Drop D," tuned down 1 1/2 steps:
⑥ = B ③ = E
⑤ = F# ② = G#
④ = B ① = C#

Lyrics by CHAD KROEGER
Music by NICKELBACK

Moderately slow ♩ = 82

Guitar → D
Piano → B
Verse:

1. There's clothes all o - ver the floor._____

3.4. *See additional lyrics*

F5
D5

Don't re - mem - ber them be - ing here be - fore._____
There's_ three_ new holes_ in the wall._____

Bb2
G2

The smell of per - fume is - n't here.
Where the hell's my cred - it cards?
Why's lip - stick on____ the mirror?
Why's my wal - let in the yard?

Should've Listened - 5 - 1
33229

And still I don't un-der-stand._____
Still I don't un-der-stand._____

| 1.

| 2.3.4.

2. No pic-tures left in the hall._____ Well, now I guess I should-'ve lis-

Chorus:

tened_ when you said you'd had e-nough._____

A lit-tle trick I picked up from my fa - ther; in__ one ear__ and out__ the oth-

A lit-tle trick I picked up from my fa - ther; in one ear__ and out__ the oth-

er. Why's love got-ta be so tough?_____

Verse 3:
Should see the look on my face.
My s***'s all over the place.
Why's this happening to mc?
Why'd you take both sets of keys?
And still I don't understand.
Well, now I guess I should've listened.
(To Chorus:)

Verse 4:
There's clothes all over my floor.
I don't remember them being there before.
There are no candles in here,
Lipstick's still on my mirror.
And still I don't understand.
And now I guess I should've listened.
(To Chorus:)

SOMEDAY

Lyrics by CHAD KROEGER
Music by NICKELBACK

Someday - 4 - 1
33229

TOO BAD

Lyrics by CHAD KROEGER
Music by NICKELBACK

Gtr. tuned down whole step
with "Drop D" tuning:
⑥ = C   ③ = F
⑤ = G   ② = A
④ = C   ① = D

Moderately ♩ = 126

Guitar ⟶ Dm
Piano ⟶ Cm

𝄋 *Verse:*

Dm
Cm

1. Fa - ther's hands—
2.4. *See additional lyrics*
3. *(Inst. solo ad lib....*

Dm/F
Cm/E♭

G2
F2

— are lined— with dirt—— from long— days in— the field.—

Dm
Cm

Dm/F
Cm/E♭

G2
F2

— Moth-er's hands—— are serv - ing meals—— in a ca-

Verse 2:
You left without saying goodbye,
Although I'm sure you tried.
You call the house from time to time
To make sure we're alive.
But you weren't there
Right when I needed you the most.
And now I dream about it,
And how it's so bad, it's so bad.
(To Chorus:)

Verse 4:
Father's hands are lined with guilt
From tearing us apart.
Guess it turned out in the end;
Just look at where we are.
We made it out;
We still got clothing on our backs.
And now I scream about it,
And how it's so bad, it's so bad,
It's so bad, it's so bad.
(To Chorus:)

IF TODAY WAS YOUR LAST DAY

Words and Music by
CHAD KROEGER

Gtr. tuned down 1/2 step:
⑥ = E♭   ③ = G♭
⑤ = A♭   ② = B♭
④ = D♭   ① = E♭

Moderately ♩ = 96

Verse:

1. My best friend gave____ me the best____ ad - vice,
2. A - gainst the grain____ should be a way____ of life,

he said each day's a gift and not a giv - en
what's worth the prize is al - ways worth the

Chorus:

and to-mor-row was__ too late,__ could you say good-bye to yes-ter-day?_

(Would you? Would you?)

Would you live each mo-ment like__ your last,__

leave old pic-tures in__ the past,__ do-nate ev-'ry dime__ you had....

1.

(Would you? Would you?)

if to-day was your__ last day?_

A
Ab

And would you find that one you're dream-ing of,____ swear up and down to God__ a-bove__

E
Eb

B
Bb

____ that you'd fi-nal-ly fall__ in love...____

(Fi-nal-ly fall in love.__

F#7(4)
F7(4)

if to-day was your__ last day?_____

Bridge:

F#5
F5

E
Eb

If to-day was your__ last day,____ would you make__ your mark__

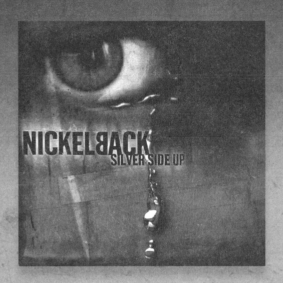

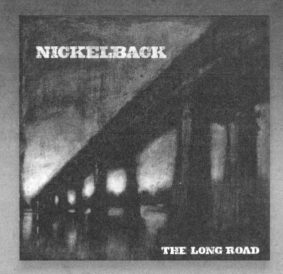

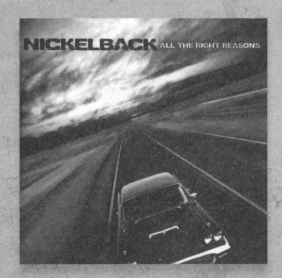

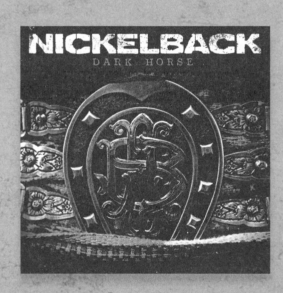